Twist, Dig, and Drill

A Book About Screws

by Michael Dahl   illustrated by Denise Shea

PICTURE WINDOW BOOKS
Minneapolis, Minnesota

Special thanks to our advisers for their expertise:

Youwen Xu, Professor
Department of Physics and Astronomy
Minnesota State University, Mankato, Minn.

Susan Kesselring, M.A.
Literacy Educator
Rosemount-Apple Valley-Eagan (Minnesota) School District

Editor: Jacqueline Wolfe
Designer: Joseph Anderson
Page Production: Melissa Kes
Creative Director: Keith Griffin
Editorial Director: Carol Jones
The illustrations in this book were created digitally.

Picture Window Books
5115 Excelsior Boulevard
Suite 232
Minneapolis, MN 55416
877-845-8392
www.picturewindowbooks.com

Printed in the United States of America.

Library of Congress Cataloging-in-Publication Data
Dahl, Michael.
Twist, dig, and drill : a book about screws / by Michael Dahl ; illustrated by
Denise Sheah.
p. cm. — (Amazing science)
Includes bibliographical references and index.
ISBN 1-4048-13063 (hard cover)
1. Screws-Juvenile literature. I. Shea, Denise. II. Title. III. Series.
TJ1338.D25 2005
621.8'82—dc22   2005024976

Table of Contents

You are sitting at the top of a gigantic water slide. Take a deep breath, push off, and plunge! Around and around you loop, lower and lower you slide. At the bottom of the slippery slope, you tumble into the pool. SPLASH! The loopy shape of the water slide is the same as a very helpful simple machine—a screw!

4

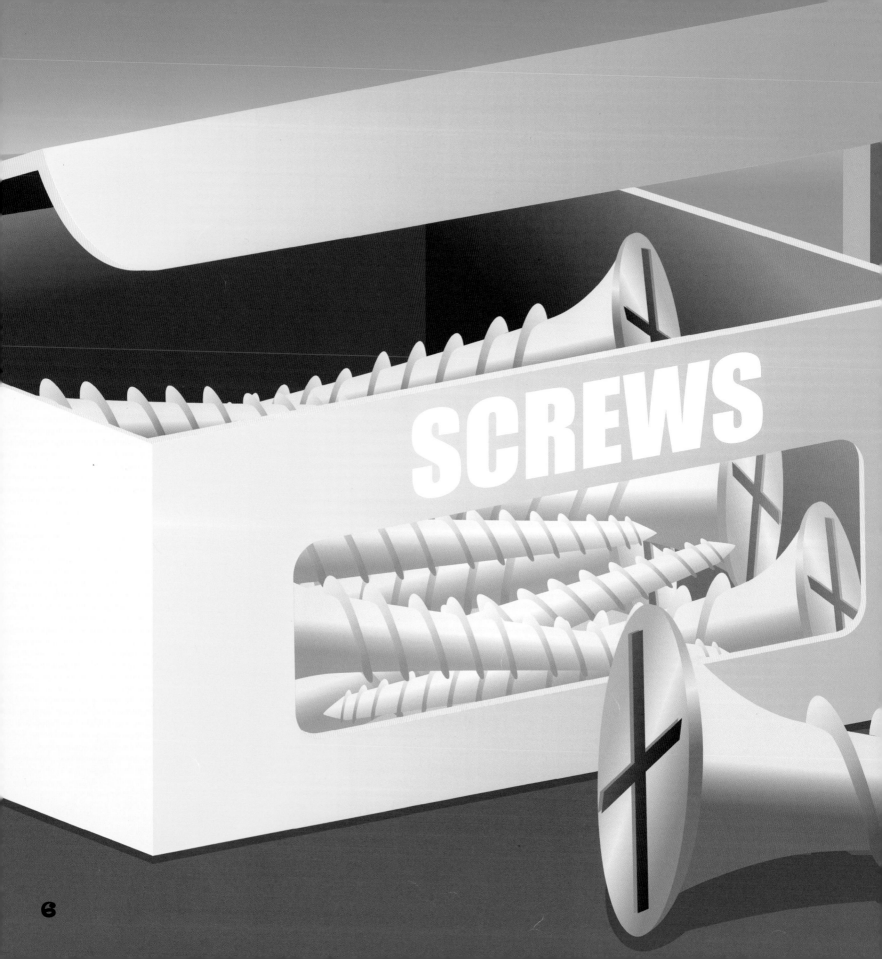

SCREWS

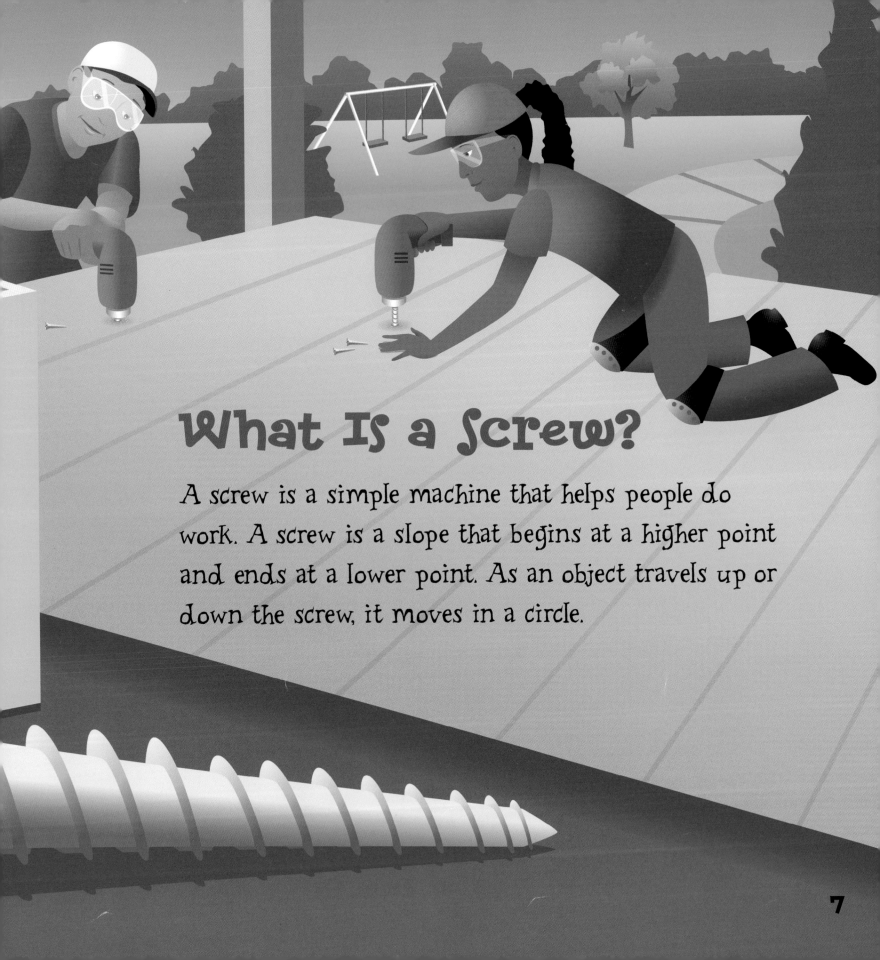

What Is a Screw?

A screw is a simple machine that helps people do work. A screw is a slope that begins at a higher point and ends at a lower point. As an object travels up or down the screw, it moves in a circle.

Screwdrivers

Screwdrivers turn small screws, pushing them into a wooden surface. As the screw twists round and round, it grabs the wood. The screw pulls the wood up its twisty, loopy body.

Soon, the head of the screw rests against the wood. The twists of the screw are still holding tightly onto the wood. Screws are good fasteners. They hold things together.

If you turn the screwdriver in the other direction, the screw twists upward, pops out, and leaves a small, round hole behind.

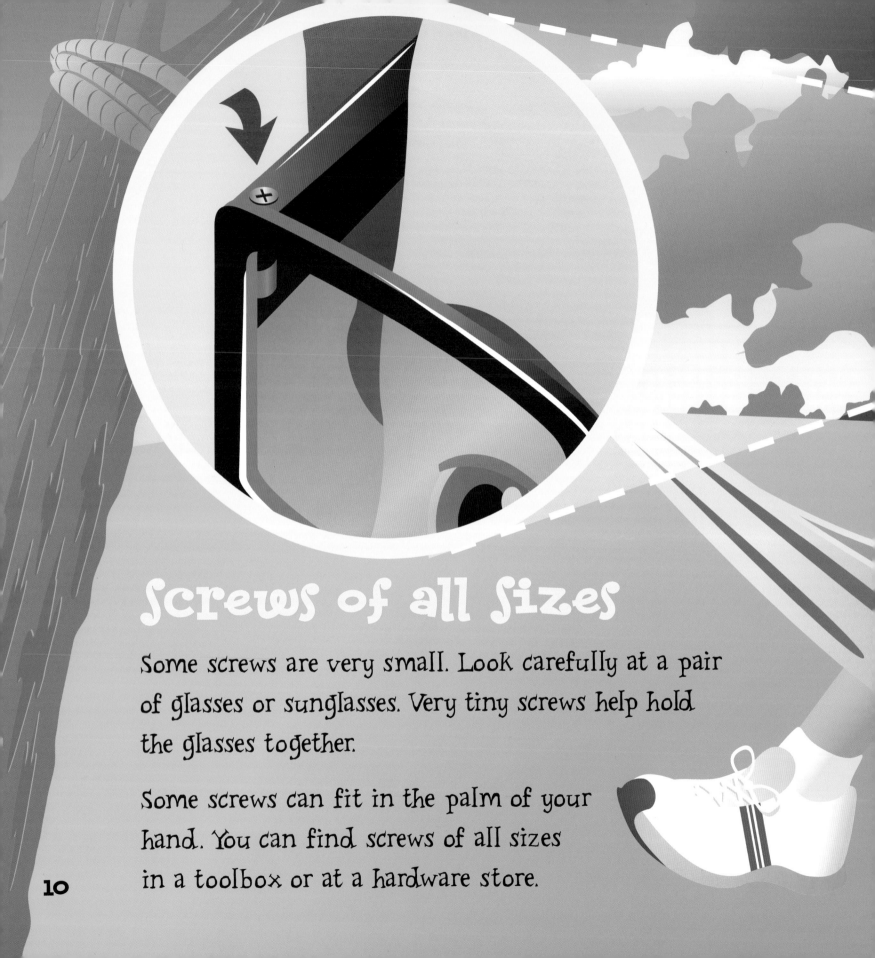

Screws of all Sizes

Some screws are very small. Look carefully at a pair of glasses or sunglasses. Very tiny screws help hold the glasses together.

Some screws can fit in the palm of your hand. You can find screws of all sizes in a toolbox or at a hardware store.

Screws for Digging

Screws can dig small holes or large, deep holes.

Augers are special screws used for digging. Augers scoop up hard soil. They gouge out deep holes for fence posts or flagpoles.

Augers also grind through thick ice. The round openings are perfect for ice fishing on large, frozen lakes.

Lids and Caps

Imagine that you want to make a snack. You open the refrigerator door to find something to eat. Many things in the refrigerator have lids or caps that have been screwed on to keep the contents fresh. Can you think of some bottles or jars in your refrigerator that have lids or caps that screw on?

Lighting It Up

Screws help you see every day. Look at the end of a lightbulb. The metal part is looped like a screw. When you twist the lightbulb to the left, it will loosen or unscrew. When you twist it to the right, it screws into the socket.

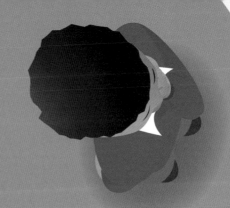

curving Up and Down

Screws can also help people move up and down inside buildings.

A curving walkway shaped like a screw twists around and around, leading visitors in a museum from floor to floor. The walkway is in the shape of a screw.

It is time to climb the ladder again. Take another plunge down the gigantic corkscrew of the water slide. Loop and twist around and around. Screws not only help people do work, they can be fun, too!

21

Up and Around: How a Screw Works

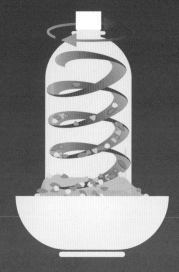

MATERIALS NEEDED:

- large plastic soda pop bottle (2 liters)
- piece of corrugated cardboard
- pencil
- scissors
- tape
- large bowl of cereal (small pieces of cereal)
- adult

WHAT YOU DO:

1. With the help of an adult, cut off the bottom of the soda pop bottle.
2. Draw a circle on the cardboard by tracing around the end of the soda pop bottle. Carefully cut out the circle.
3. Put a small dot in the middle of the cardboard circle. Draw a spiral from the edge of the cardboard circle to dot. Carefully cut along the spiral.
4. Hold the circle at the end where the dot was. The other end will hang down in a spiral. The cardboard circle now hangs in the shape of a screw.
5. Tape the screw shape inside the bottle.
6. Put the cut end of the bottle into the bowl of cereal.
7. Slowly turn the bottle. The cereal should travel up the screw to the top of the bottle. If it doesn't work, try turning the bottle in the opposite direction.

FOLLOW UP QUESTIONS:

1. What other things could you make swirl up the screw?
2. Do you think this could work with a bigger bottle? Smaller bottle?

fun facts

Around the first century, screw-shaped tools became common. However, historians do not know who invented the first one.

Most early screws were made from wood.

There are many different types of screw heads including Pan head, Cheese head, and button (or dome) head.

An easy way to remember which direction will screw or unscrew a screw is to remember that turning it LEFT will LOOSEN. Remember that they both start with the letter "L."

Boring is another word for digging something out with a screw.

Glossary

auger—special screws used to dig through hard soil and ice
screw—a simple machine with a nail or rod shape
      with a spiral groove
screwdriver—a tool for turning screws
simple machine—a machine that helps people do work
slope—upward or downward slant
socket—the part of a light fixture the lightbulb is screwed into

To Learn More

AT THE LIBRARY

Douglas, Lloyd G. *What Is a Plane?* New York:
  Children's Press, 2002.

Mason, Adrienne & Deborah Hodge. *Simple
  Machines.* New York: Kids Can Press, 2000.

Oxlade, Chris. *Ramps and Wedges.* Chicago, Ill.
  Heinemann, 2003.

ON THE WEB

FactHound offers a safe, fun way to find Internet
sites related to this book. All of the sites on
FactHound have been researched by our staff.

1. Visit *www.facthound.com*
2. Type in this special code for age-appropriate
   sites: *1404813063*
3. Click on the FETCH IT button. Your trusty
   FactHound will fetch the best sites for you!

LOOK FOR ALL OF THE BOOKS IN THE AMAZING SCIENCE SERIES:

Air: Outside, Inside, and All Around	1-4048-0248-7	Pull, Lift, and Lower: A Book About Pulleys	1-4048-1305-5
Cut, Chop, and Stop: A Book About Wedges	1-4048-1307-1	Rocks: Hard, Soft, Smooth, and Rough	1-4048-0015-8
Dirt: The Scoop on Soil	1-4048-0012-3	Roll, Slope, and Slide: A Book About Ramps	1-4048-1304-7
Electricity: Bulbs, Batteries, and Sparks	1-4048-0245-2	Scoop, Seesaw, and Raise: A Book About Levers	1-4048-1303-9
Energy: Heat, Light, and Fuel	1-4048-0249-5	Sound: Loud, Soft, High, and Low	1-4048-0016-6
Light: Shadows, Mirrors, and Rainbows	1-4048-0013-1	Temperature: Heating Up and Cooling Down	1-4048-0247-9
Magnets: Pulling Together, Pushing Apart	1-4048-0014-X	Tires, Spokes, and Sprockets: A Book About Wheels	1-4048-1308-X
Matter: See It, Touch It, Taste It, Smell It	1-4048-0246-0	Twist, Dig, and Drill: A Book About Screws	1-4048-1306-3
Motion: Push and Pull, Fast and Slow	1-4048-0250-9	Water: Up, Down, and All Around	14048-0017-4a